ST. JOSEPH THE WORKER

A NINE-DAY PRAYER AND MANDATE OF ST. JOSEPH NOVENA

Beatrix.C.Brown

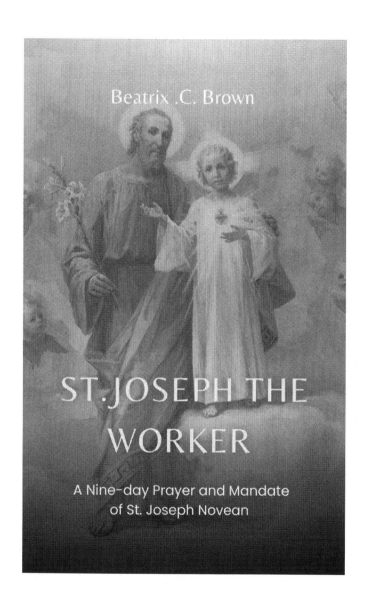

Beatrix .C. Brown

ST.JOSEPH THE WORKER

A Nine-day Prayer and Mandate
of St. Joseph Novean

Table of contents

Brief History of ST. JOSEPH

ST JOSEPH THE WORKER, SPOUSE OF THE BLESSED VIRGIN MARY, PATRON OF WORKERS

In addition to being the husband of the Blessed Virgin Mary, and the foster-father of Jesus, St Joseph was a carpenter. Through his job of physical labor, Joseph supplied for the Holy Family, and joined in the divine plan of redemption.

Joseph the " Just man"

The Gospel of St Matthew defines Joseph as a "just man", which in the language of the Bible indicates one who loves and respects the law as the manifestation of the will of God. Like Mary, Joseph too was visited by an angel, who came to him in a dream. And, just like Mary, her husband, Joseph responded "Yes", when the angel revealed that the Child she carried was conceived by the Holy Spirit.The particular trait of Joseph is hiddenness, staying in the background. No mention of his is preserved in the Gospels. He is not mentioned following the discovery of Christ in the Temple.

Probably by the time Jesus started his public existence, at the wedding in Cana, Joseph had already departed to the next life, although we don't know precisely when or where he died. And the spot of his interment remains a mystery.

Work: Participation in the Divine Plan

As is typical of many fathers, Joseph raised Jesus to follow in his own trade as a craftsman; in the Gospels, Jesus is dubbed **"the son of the carpenter"**.

The life of St Joseph teaches us the dignity of human activity, which is the responsibility and the perfection of human beings, who in this manner exercise dominion over creation, join in the work of the Creator, give their contribution to the community, and participate in God's plan of redemption. Joseph enjoyed his job. He never complained of tiredness, but as a man of faith raised it to the practice of virtue. He found pleasure in his job,because he did not strive to money and did not envy the affluent; for Joseph, labor was not a way to fulfill his personal greed, but an instrument to sustain his family.And, following God's instruction, on the Sabbath St Joseph observed the weekly rest and took part in the festivities. We should not marvel at this magnificent idea of the modest labor of physical labor: since in the Old Testament, in fact, God was viewed figuratively as a winegrower, a sower, a shepherd.

The feast of Saint Joseph the Worker

This feast was formally created by Pope Pius XII on 1 May 1955, in order to guarantee that workers not lose this Christian concept of labor; although prior Popes had already set the basis. Blessed Pius IX in a certain sense had acknowledged the value of Saint Joseph as a worker, when he designated him Patron of the Universal Church. The notion of labour as a route to everlasting salvation would be taken up again by St John Paul II in his encyclical Laborem exercens, where he alludes to "the Gospel of Work ". And Cardinal Angelo Roncalli – who became Pope St John XXIII – when he was elected to the Throne of Peter had thought of choosing the name Joseph, so dedicated was he to the saint who was the foster-father of Jesus. Many other saints, like St Teresa of Avila, have a particular devotion to Saint Joseph.

St Joseph represents the true model of work for Catholics and all people, since he had the supreme honor of working with Jesus Christ in the carpenter shop at Nazareth. Pray for this novena for finding a job and for help with your work.

You can pray the full St Joseph the Worker Novena below.

Day 1 Prayer

In the name of the Father, and of the Son, and of the Holy Spirit. Amen.

Intro Prayer
Dear Saint Joseph, I praise God for the honor of being able to labor side-by-side with Jesus in the carpenter shop of Nazareth.

As a mark of thine own appreciation to God, gain for me the grace to appreciate the dignity of work and ever to be satisfied with the situation in life, however humble, in which it may please Divine Providence to set me.

Teach me to labor for God and with God in the spirit of humility and prayer, as thou did, so that I may give my toil in connection with the sacrifice of Jesus in the Holy Mass as a restitution for my sins, and acquire great merit for heaven.

St Joseph, I, your worthless child, welcome thee. Thou are the loyal guardian and intercessor of those who love and revere thee.

Thou knowest that I have great trust in thee and that, after Our Lord and Our Lady, I invest all my hope of salvation in thee, because thou art exceptionally

strong with God and wilt never desert thy devoted followers.

Therefore I humbly implore thee and commit myself, with those who are dear to me and everything that pertains to me, to thy intercession.

I implore thee, by thy love for Our Lord and Our Lady, not to desert me throughout life and to aid me at the hour of my death. Glorious Saint Joseph, husband of the Immaculate Virgin, gain for me a pure, modest, generous spirit and full surrender to the divine Will. Be my guide, my father and my model through life so I may deserve to die as Thou didst in the arms of Our Lord and Our Lady.

Loving Saint Joseph, faithful follower of Jesus Christ, I raise my heart to thee to implore thy powerful intercession in obtaining from the Divine Heart of Jesus all the graces necessary for my spiritual and temporal welfare, particularly the grace of a happy death and the special grace I now implore:

(Mention your desire).

Guardian of the Word Incarnate, I am certain that thy petitions on my behalf will be mercifully received before the throne of God. Amen.

Remember, most pure husband of Mary, eternally Virgin, my beloved defender, Saint Joseph, that no

one ever had recourse to thy protection or begged for thy help without gaining relief. Confiding, then, on thy benevolence, I stand before thee and humbly entreat thee. Despise not my requests, foster-father of the Redeemer, but kindly welcome them. Amen.

Concluding Prayer

Pope Leo XIII's Prayer to St Joseph (from Quamquam Pluries)

To thee, O blessed Joseph, we have recourse in our affliction, and having implored the help of thy thrice holy Spouse, we now, with hearts filled with confidence, earnestly beg thee also to take us under thy protection.

By that charity wherewith thou wert united to the Immaculate Virgin Mother of God, and by that fatherly love with which thou didst cherish the Child Jesus, we beseech thee and we humbly pray that thou wilt look down with gracious eye upon that inheritance which Jesus Christ purchased by His blood, and wilt succor us in our need by thy power and strength.

Defend, O most watchful guardian of the Holy Family, the chosen off-spring of Jesus Christ. Keep from us, O most loving Father, all blight of error and corruption. Aid us from on high, most valiant defender, in this conflict with the powers of darkness.

And even as of old thou didst rescue the Child Jesus from the peril of His life, so now defend God's Holy Church from the snares of the enemy and from all adversity. Shield us ever under thy patronage, that, following thine example and strengthened by thy help, we may live a holy life, die a happy death, and attain everlasting bliss in Heaven. Amen.

Day 2 Prayer

In the name of the Father, and of the Son, and of the Holy Spirit. Amen.

Intro Prayer

Dear Saint Joseph, I praise God for the honor of being able to labor side-by-side with Jesus in the carpenter shop of Nazareth.

As a mark of thine own appreciation to God, gain for me the grace to appreciate the dignity of work and ever to be satisfied with the situation in life, however humble, in which it may please Divine Providence to set me.

Teach me to labor for God and with God in the spirit of humility and prayer, as thou did, so that I may give my toil in connection with the sacrifice of Jesus in the Holy Mass as a restitution for my sins, and acquire great merit for heaven.

St Joseph, I, your worthless child, welcome thee. Thou are the loyal guardian and intercessor of those who love and revere thee.

Thou knowest that I have great trust in thee and that, after Our Lord and Our Lady, I invest all my hope of salvation in thee, because thou art exceptionally

strong with God and wilt never desert thy devoted followers.

Therefore I humbly implore thee and commit myself, with those who are dear to me and everything that pertains to me, to thy intercession.

I implore thee, by thy love for Our Lord and Our Lady, not to desert me throughout life and to aid me at the hour of my death. Glorious Saint Joseph, husband of the Immaculate Virgin, gain for me a pure, modest, generous spirit and full surrender to the divine Will. Be my guide, my father and my model through life so I may deserve to die as Thou didst in the arms of Our Lord and Our Lady.

Loving Saint Joseph, faithful follower of Jesus Christ, I raise my heart to thee to implore thy powerful intercession in obtaining from the Divine Heart of Jesus all the graces necessary for my spiritual and temporal welfare, particularly the grace of a happy death and the special grace I now implore:

(Mention your desire).

Guardian of the Word Incarnate, I am certain that thy petitions on my behalf will be mercifully received before the throne of God. Amen.

Remember, most pure husband of Mary, eternally Virgin, my beloved defender, Saint Joseph, that no

one ever had recourse to thy protection or begged for thy help without gaining relief. Confiding, then, on thy benevolence, I stand before thee and humbly entreat thee. Despise not my requests, foster-father of the Redeemer, but kindly welcome them. Amen.

Concluding Prayer

Pope Leo XIII's Prayer to St Joseph (from Quamquam Pluries)

To thee, O blessed Joseph, we have recourse in our affliction, and having implored the help of thy thrice holy Spouse, we now, with hearts filled with confidence, earnestly beg thee also to take us under thy protection.

By that charity wherewith thou wert united to the Immaculate Virgin Mother of God, and by that fatherly love with which thou didst cherish the Child Jesus, we beseech thee and we humbly pray that thou wilt look down with gracious eye upon that inheritance which Jesus Christ purchased by His blood, and wilt succor us in our need by thy power and strength.

Defend, O most watchful guardian of the Holy Family, the chosen off-spring of Jesus Christ. Keep from us, O most loving Father, all blight of error and corruption. Aid us from on high, most valiant defender, in this conflict with the powers of darkness.

And even as of old thou didst rescue the Child Jesus from the peril of His life, so now defend God's Holy Church from the snares of the enemy and from all adversity. Shield us ever under thy patronage, that, following thine example and strengthened by thy help, we may live a holy life, die a happy death, and attain to everlasting bliss in Heaven. Amen.

Day 3 Prayer

In the name of the Father, and of the Son, and of the Holy Spirit. Amen.

Intro Prayer

Dear Saint Joseph, I praise God for the honor of being able to labor side-by-side with Jesus in the carpenter shop of Nazareth.

As a mark of thine own appreciation to God, gain for me the grace to appreciate the dignity of work and ever to be satisfied with the situation in life, however humble, in which it may please Divine Providence to set me.

Teach me to labor for God and with God in the spirit of humility and prayer, as thou did, so that I may give my toil in connection with the sacrifice of Jesus in the Holy Mass as a restitution for my sins, and acquire great merit for heaven.

St Joseph, I, your worthless child, welcome thee. Thou are the loyal guardian and intercessor of those who love and revere thee.

Thou knowest that I have great trust in thee and that, after Our Lord and Our Lady, I invest all my hope of salvation in thee, because thou art exceptionally strong with God and wilt never desert thy devoted followers.

Therefore I humbly implore thee and commit myself, with those who are dear to me and everything that pertains to me, to thy intercession.

I implore thee, by thy love for Our Lord and Our Lady, not to desert me throughout life and to aid me at the hour of my death. Glorious Saint Joseph, husband of the Immaculate Virgin, gain for me a pure, modest, generous spirit and full surrender to the divine Will. Be my guide, my father and my model through life so I may deserve to die as Thou didst in the arms of Our Lord and Our Lady.

Loving Saint Joseph, faithful follower of Jesus Christ, I raise my heart to thee to implore thy powerful intercession in obtaining from the Divine Heart of Jesus all the graces necessary for my spiritual and temporal welfare, particularly the grace of a happy death and the special grace I now implore:

(Mention your desire).

Guardian of the Word Incarnate, I am certain that thy petitions on my behalf will be mercifully received before the throne of God. Amen.

Remember, most pure husband of Mary, eternally Virgin, my beloved defender, Saint Joseph, that no one ever had recourse to thy protection or begged for thy help without gaining relief. Confiding, then, on

thy benevolence, I stand before thee and humbly entreat thee. Despise not my requests, foster-father of the Redeemer, but kindly welcome them. Amen.

Concluding Prayer

Pope Leo XIII's Prayer to St Joseph (from Quamquam Pluries)

To thee, O blessed Joseph, we have recourse in our affliction, and having implored the help of thy thrice holy Spouse, we now, with hearts filled with confidence, earnestly beg thee also to take us under thy protection.

By that charity wherewith thou wert united to the Immaculate Virgin Mother of God, and by that fatherly love with which thou didst cherish the Child Jesus, we beseech thee and we humbly pray that thou wilt look down with gracious eye upon that inheritance which Jesus Christ purchased by His blood, and wilt succor us in our need by thy power and strength.

Defend, O most watchful guardian of the Holy Family, the chosen off-spring of Jesus Christ. Keep from us, O most loving Father, all blight of error and corruption. Aid us from on high, most valiant defender, in this conflict with the powers of darkness.

And even as of old thou didst rescue the Child Jesus from the peril of His life, so now defend God's Holy

Church from the snares of the enemy and from all adversity. Shield us ever under thy patronage, that, following thine example and strengthened by thy help, we may live a holy life, die a happy death, and attain to everlasting bliss in Heaven. Amen.

Day 4 Prayer

In the name of the Father, and of the Son, and of the Holy Spirit. Amen.

Intro Prayer
Dear Saint Joseph, I praise God for the honor of being able to labor side-by-side with Jesus in the carpenter shop of Nazareth.

As a mark of thine own appreciation to God, gain for me the grace to appreciate the dignity of work and ever to be satisfied with the situation in life, however humble, in which it may please Divine Providence to set me.

Teach me to labor for God and with God in the spirit of humility and prayer, as thou did, so that I may give my toil in connection with the sacrifice of Jesus in the Holy Mass as a restitution for my sins, and acquire great merit for heaven.

St Joseph, I, your worthless child, welcome thee. Thou are the loyal guardian and intercessor of those who love and revere thee.

Thou knowest that I have great trust in thee and that, after Our Lord and Our Lady, I invest all my hope of salvation in thee, because thou art exceptionally strong with God and wilt never desert thy devoted followers.

Therefore I humbly implore thee and commit myself, with those who are dear to me and everything that pertains to me, to thy intercession.

I implore thee, by thy love for Our Lord and Our Lady, not to desert me throughout life and to aid me at the hour of my death. Glorious Saint Joseph, husband of the Immaculate Virgin, gain for me a pure, modest, generous spirit and full surrender to the divine Will. Be my guide, my father and my model through life so I may deserve to die as Thou didst in the arms of Our Lord and Our Lady.

Loving Saint Joseph, faithful follower of Jesus Christ, I raise my heart to thee to implore thy powerful intercession in obtaining from the Divine Heart of Jesus all the graces necessary for my spiritual and temporal welfare, particularly the grace of a happy death and the special grace I now implore:

(Mention your desire).

Guardian of the Word Incarnate, I am certain that thy petitions on my behalf will be mercifully received before the throne of God. Amen.

Remember, most pure husband of Mary, eternally Virgin, my beloved defender, Saint Joseph, that no one ever had recourse to thy protection or begged for thy help without gaining relief. Confiding, then, on

thy benevolence, I stand before thee and humbly entreat thee. Despise not my requests, foster-father of the Redeemer, but kindly welcome them. Amen.

Concluding Prayer

Pope Leo XIII's Prayer to St Joseph (from Quamquam Pluries)

To thee, O blessed Joseph, we have recourse in our affliction, and having implored the help of thy thrice holy Spouse, we now, with hearts filled with confidence, earnestly beg thee also to take us under thy protection.

By that charity wherewith thou wert united to the Immaculate Virgin Mother of God, and by that fatherly love with which thou didst cherish the Child Jesus, we beseech thee and we humbly pray that thou wilt look down with gracious eye upon that inheritance which Jesus Christ purchased by His blood, and wilt succor us in our need by thy power and strength.

Defend, O most watchful guardian of the Holy Family, the chosen off-spring of Jesus Christ. Keep from us, O most loving Father, all blight of error and corruption. Aid us from on high, most valiant defender, in this conflict with the powers of darkness.

And even as of old thou didst rescue the Child Jesus from the peril of His life, so now defend God's Holy

Church from the snares of the enemy and from all adversity. Shield us ever under thy patronage, that, following thine example and strengthened by thy help, we may live a holy life, die a happy death, and attain to everlasting bliss in Heaven. Amen.

Day 5 Prayer

In the name of the Father, and of the Son, and of the Holy Spirit. Amen.

Intro Prayer

Dear Saint Joseph, I praise God for the honor of being able to labor side-by-side with Jesus in the carpenter shop of Nazareth.

As a mark of thine own appreciation to God, gain for me the grace to appreciate the dignity of work and ever to be satisfied with the situation in life, however humble, in which it may please Divine Providence to set me.

Teach me to labor for God and with God in the spirit of humility and prayer, as thou did, so that I may give my toil in connection with the sacrifice of Jesus in the Holy Mass as a restitution for my sins, and acquire great merit for heaven.

St Joseph, I, your worthless child, welcome thee. Thou are the loyal guardian and intercessor of those who love and revere thee.

Thou knowest that I have great trust in thee and that, after Our Lord and Our Lady, I invest all my hope of salvation in thee, because thou art exceptionally strong with God and wilt never desert thy devoted followers.

Therefore I humbly implore thee and commit myself, with those who are dear to me and everything that pertains to me, to thy intercession.

I implore thee, by thy love for Our Lord and Our Lady, not to desert me throughout life and to aid me at the hour of my death. Glorious Saint Joseph, husband of the Immaculate Virgin, gain for me a pure, modest, generous spirit and full surrender to the divine Will. Be my guide, my father and my model through life so I may deserve to die as Thou didst in the arms of Our Lord and Our Lady.

Loving Saint Joseph, faithful follower of Jesus Christ, I raise my heart to thee to implore thy powerful intercession in obtaining from the Divine Heart of Jesus all the graces necessary for my spiritual and temporal welfare, particularly the grace of a happy death and the special grace I now implore:

(Mention your desire).

Guardian of the Word Incarnate, I am certain that thy petitions on my behalf will be mercifully received before the throne of God. Amen.

Remember, most pure husband of Mary, eternally Virgin, my beloved defender, Saint Joseph, that no one ever had recourse to thy protection or begged for thy help without gaining relief. Confiding, then, on

thy benevolence, I stand before thee and humbly entreat thee. Despise not my requests, foster-father of the Redeemer, but kindly welcome them. Amen.

Concluding Prayer

Pope Leo XIII's Prayer to St Joseph (from Quamquam Pluries)

To thee, O blessed Joseph, we have recourse in our affliction, and having implored the help of thy thrice holy Spouse, we now, with hearts filled with confidence, earnestly beg thee also to take us under thy protection.

By that charity wherewith thou wert united to the Immaculate Virgin Mother of God, and by that fatherly love with which thou didst cherish the Child Jesus, we beseech thee and we humbly pray that thou wilt look down with gracious eye upon that inheritance which Jesus Christ purchased by His blood, and wilt succor us in our need by thy power and strength.

Defend, O most watchful guardian of the Holy Family, the chosen off-spring of Jesus Christ. Keep from us, O most loving Father, all blight of error and corruption. Aid us from on high, most valiant defender, in this conflict with the powers of darkness.

And even as of old thou didst rescue the Child Jesus from the peril of His life, so now defend God's Holy

Church from the snares of the enemy and from all adversity. Shield us ever under thy patronage, that, following thine example and strengthened by thy help, we may live a holy life, die a happy death, and attain everlasting bliss in Heaven. Amen.

Day 6 prayer

In the name of the Father, and of the Son, and of the Holy Spirit. Amen.

Intro Prayer

Dear Saint Joseph, I praise God for the honor of being able to labor side-by-side with Jesus in the carpenter shop of Nazareth.

As a mark of thine own appreciation to God, gain for me the grace to appreciate the dignity of work and ever to be satisfied with the situation in life, however humble, in which it may please Divine Providence to set me.

Teach me to labor for God and with God in the spirit of humility and prayer, as thou did, so that I may give my toil in connection with the sacrifice of Jesus in the Holy Mass as a restitution for my sins, and acquire great merit for heaven.

St Joseph, I, your worthless child, welcome thee. Thou are the loyal guardian and intercessor of those who love and revere thee.

Thou knowest that I have great trust in thee and that, after Our Lord and Our Lady, I invest all my hope of salvation in thee, because thou art exceptionally strong with God and wilt never desert thy devoted followers.

Therefore I humbly implore thee and commit myself, with those who are dear to me and everything that pertains to me, to thy intercession.

I implore thee, by thy love for Our Lord and Our Lady, not to desert me throughout life and to aid me at the hour of my death. Glorious Saint Joseph, husband of the Immaculate Virgin, gain for me a pure, modest, generous spirit and full surrender to the divine Will. Be my guide, my father and my model through life so I may deserve to die as Thou didst in the arms of Our Lord and Our Lady.

Loving Saint Joseph, faithful follower of Jesus Christ, I raise my heart to thee to implore thy powerful intercession in obtaining from the Divine Heart of Jesus all the graces necessary for my spiritual and temporal welfare, particularly the grace of a happy death and the special grace I now implore:

(Mention your desire).

Guardian of the Word Incarnate, I am certain that thy petitions on my behalf will be mercifully received before the throne of God. Amen.

Remember, most pure husband of Mary, eternally Virgin, my beloved defender, Saint Joseph, that no one ever had recourse to thy protection or begged for thy help without gaining relief. Confiding, then, on

thy benevolence, I stand before thee and humbly entreat thee. Despise not my requests, foster-father of the Redeemer, but kindly welcome them. Amen.

Concluding Prayer

Pope Leo XIII's Prayer to St Joseph (from Quamquam Pluries)

To thee, O blessed Joseph, we have recourse in our affliction, and having implored the help of thy thrice holy Spouse, we now, with hearts filled with confidence, earnestly beg thee also to take us under thy protection.

By that charity wherewith thou wert united to the Immaculate Virgin Mother of God, and by that fatherly love with which thou didst cherish the Child Jesus, we beseech thee and we humbly pray that thou wilt look down with gracious eye upon that inheritance which Jesus Christ purchased by His blood, and wilt succor us in our need by thy power and strength.

Defend, O most watchful guardian of the Holy Family, the chosen off-spring of Jesus Christ. Keep from us, O most loving Father, all blight of error and corruption. Aid us from on high, most valiant defender, in this conflict with the powers of darkness.

And even as of old thou didst rescue the Child Jesus from the peril of His life, so now defend God's Holy

Church from the snares of the enemy and from all adversity. Shield us ever under thy patronage, that, following thine example and strengthened by thy help, we may live a holy life, die a happy death, and attain to everlasting bliss in Heaven. Amen.

Day 7 prayer

In the name of the Father, and of the Son, and of the Holy Spirit. Amen.

Intro Prayer

Dear Saint Joseph, I praise God for the honor of being able to labor side-by-side with Jesus in the carpenter shop of Nazareth.

As a mark of thine own appreciation to God, gain for me the grace to appreciate the dignity of work and ever to be satisfied with the situation in life, however humble, in which it may please Divine Providence to set me.

Teach me to labor for God and with God in the spirit of humility and prayer, as thou did, so that I may give my toil in connection with the sacrifice of Jesus in the Holy Mass as a restitution for my sins, and acquire great merit for heaven.

St Joseph, I, your worthless child, welcome thee. Thou are the loyal guardian and intercessor of those who love and revere thee.

Thou knowest that I have great trust in thee and that, after Our Lord and Our Lady, I invest all my hope of salvation in thee, because thou art exceptionally

strong with God and wilt never desert thy devoted followers.

Therefore I humbly implore thee and commit myself, with those who are dear to me and everything that pertains to me, to thy intercession.

I implore thee, by thy love for Our Lord and Our Lady, not to desert me throughout life and to aid me at the hour of my death. Glorious Saint Joseph, husband of the Immaculate Virgin, gain for me a pure, modest, generous spirit and full surrender to the divine Will. Be my guide, my father and my model through life so I may deserve to die as Thou didst in the arms of Our Lord and Our Lady.

Loving Saint Joseph, faithful follower of Jesus Christ, I raise my heart to thee to implore thy powerful intercession in obtaining from the Divine Heart of Jesus all the graces necessary for my spiritual and temporal welfare, particularly the grace of a happy death and the special grace I now implore:

(Mention your desire).

Guardian of the Word Incarnate, I am certain that thy petitions on my behalf will be mercifully received before the throne of God. Amen.

Remember, most pure husband of Mary, eternally Virgin, my beloved defender, Saint Joseph, that no

one ever had recourse to thy protection or begged for thy help without gaining relief. Confiding, then, on thy benevolence, I stand before thee and humbly entreat thee. Despise not my requests, foster-father of the Redeemer, but kindly welcome them. Amen.

Concluding Prayer

Pope Leo XIII's Prayer to St Joseph (from Quamquam Pluries)

To thee, O blessed Joseph, we have recourse in our affliction, and having implored the help of thy thrice holy Spouse, we now, with hearts filled with confidence, earnestly beg thee also to take us under thy protection.

By that charity wherewith thou wert united to the Immaculate Virgin Mother of God, and by that fatherly love with which thou didst cherish the Child Jesus, we beseech thee and we humbly pray that thou wilt look down with gracious eye upon that inheritance which Jesus Christ purchased by His blood, and wilt succor us in our need by thy power and strength.

Defend, O most watchful guardian of the Holy Family, the chosen off-spring of Jesus Christ. Keep from us, O most loving Father, all blight of error and corruption. Aid us from on high, most valiant defender, in this conflict with the powers of darkness.

And even as of old thou didst rescue the Child Jesus from the peril of His life, so now defend God's Holy Church from the snares of the enemy and from all adversity. Shield us ever under thy patronage, that, following thine example and strengthened by thy help, we may live a holy life, die a happy death, and attain to everlasting bliss in Heaven. Amen.

Day 8 prayer

In the name of the Father, and of the Son, and of the Holy Spirit. Amen.

Intro Prayer

Dear Saint Joseph, I praise God for the honor of being able to labor side-by-side with Jesus in the carpenter shop of Nazareth.

As a mark of thine own appreciation to God, gain for me the grace to appreciate the dignity of work and ever to be satisfied with the situation in life, however humble, in which it may please Divine Providence to set me.

Teach me to labor for God and with God in the spirit of humility and prayer, as thou did, so that I may give my toil in connection with the sacrifice of Jesus in the Holy Mass as a restitution for my sins, and acquire great merit for heaven.

St Joseph, I, your worthless child, welcome thee. Thou are the loyal guardian and intercessor of those who love and revere thee.

Thou knowest that I have great trust in thee and that, after Our Lord and Our Lady, I invest all my hope of salvation in thee, because thou art exceptionally strong with God and wilt never desert thy devoted followers.

Therefore I humbly implore thee and commit myself, with those who are dear to me and everything that pertains to me, to thy intercession.

I implore thee, by thy love for Our Lord and Our Lady, not to desert me throughout life and to aid me at the hour of my death. Glorious Saint Joseph, husband of the Immaculate Virgin, gain for me a pure, modest, generous spirit and full surrender to the divine Will. Be my guide, my father and my model through life so I may deserve to die as Thou didst in the arms of Our Lord and Our Lady.

Loving Saint Joseph, faithful follower of Jesus Christ, I raise my heart to thee to implore thy powerful intercession in obtaining from the Divine Heart of Jesus all the graces necessary for my spiritual and temporal welfare, particularly the grace of a happy death and the special grace I now implore:

(Mention your desire).

Guardian of the Word Incarnate, I am certain that thy petitions on my behalf will be mercifully received before the throne of God. Amen.

Remember, most pure husband of Mary, eternally Virgin, my beloved defender, Saint Joseph, that no one ever had recourse to thy protection or begged for thy help without gaining relief. Confiding, then, on

thy benevolence, I stand before thee and humbly entreat thee. Despise not my requests, foster-father of the Redeemer, but kindly welcome them. Amen.

Concluding Prayer

Pope Leo XIII's Prayer to St Joseph (from Quamquam Pluries)

To thee, O blessed Joseph, we have recourse in our affliction, and having implored the help of thy thrice holy Spouse, we now, with hearts filled with confidence, earnestly beg thee also to take us under thy protection.

By that charity wherewith thou wert united to the Immaculate Virgin Mother of God, and by that fatherly love with which thou didst cherish the Child Jesus, we beseech thee and we humbly pray that thou wilt look down with gracious eye upon that inheritance which Jesus Christ purchased by His blood, and wilt succor us in our need by thy power and strength.

Defend, O most watchful guardian of the Holy Family, the chosen off-spring of Jesus Christ. Keep from us, O most loving Father, all blight of error and corruption. Aid us from on high, most valiant defender, in this conflict with the powers of darkness.

And even as of old thou didst rescue the Child Jesus from the peril of His life, so now defend God's Holy

Church from the snares of the enemy and from all adversity. Shield us ever under thy patronage, that, following thine example and strengthened by thy help, we may live a holy life, die a happy death, and attain to everlasting bliss in Heaven. Amen.

Day 9 prayer

In the name of the Father, and of the Son, and of the Holy Spirit. Amen.

Intro Prayer

Dear Saint Joseph, I praise God for the honor of being able to labor side-by-side with Jesus in the carpenter shop of Nazareth.

As a mark of thine own appreciation to God, gain for me the grace to appreciate the dignity of work and ever to be satisfied with the situation in life, however humble, in which it may please Divine Providence to set me.

Teach me to labor for God and with God in the spirit of humility and prayer, as thou did, so that I may give my toil in connection with the sacrifice of Jesus in the Holy Mass as a restitution for my sins, and acquire great merit for heaven.

St Joseph, I, your worthless child, welcome thee. Thou are the loyal guardian and intercessor of those who love and revere thee.

Thou knowest that I have great trust in thee and that, after Our Lord and Our Lady, I invest all my hope of salvation in thee, because thou art exceptionally strong with God and wilt never desert thy devoted followers.

Therefore I humbly implore thee and commit myself, with those who are dear to me and everything that pertains to me, to thy intercession.

I implore thee, by thy love for Our Lord and Our Lady, not to desert me throughout life and to aid me at the hour of my death. Glorious Saint Joseph, husband of the Immaculate Virgin, gained for me a pure, modest, generous spirit and full surrender to the divine Will. Be my guide, my father and my model through life so I may deserve to die as Thou didst in the arms of Our Lord and Our Lady.

Loving Saint Joseph, faithful follower of Jesus Christ, I raise my heart to thee to implore thy powerful intercession in obtaining from the Divine Heart of Jesus all the graces necessary for my spiritual and temporal welfare, particularly the grace of a happy death and the special grace I now implore:

(Mention your desire).

Guardian of the Word Incarnate, I am certain that thy petitions on my behalf will be mercifully received before the throne of God. Amen.

Remember, most pure husband of Mary, eternally Virgin, my beloved defender, Saint Joseph, that no one ever had recourse to thy protection or begged for thy help without gaining relief. Confiding, then, on

thy benevolence, I stand before thee and humbly entreat thee. Despise not my requests, foster-father of the Redeemer, but kindly welcome them. Amen.

Concluding Prayer

Pope Leo XIII's Prayer to St Joseph (from Quamquam Pluries)

To thee, O blessed Joseph, we have recourse in our affliction, and having implored the help of thy thrice holy Spouse, we now, with hearts filled with confidence, earnestly beg thee also to take us under thy protection.

By that charity wherewith thou wert united to the Immaculate Virgin Mother of God, and by that fatherly love with which thou didst cherish the Child Jesus, we beseech thee and we humbly pray that thou wilt look down with gracious eye upon that inheritance which Jesus Christ purchased by His blood, and wilt succor us in our need by thy power and strength.

Defend, O most watchful guardian of the Holy Family, the chosen off-spring of Jesus Christ. Keep from us, O most loving Father, all blight of error and corruption. Aid us from on high, most valiant defender, in this conflict with the powers of darkness.

And even as of old thou didst rescue the Child Jesus from the peril of His life, so now defend God's Holy

Church from the snares of the enemy and from all adversity. Shield us ever under thy patronage, that, following thine example and strengthened by thy help, we may live a holy life, die a happy death, and attain to everlasting bliss in Heaven. Amen.

PRAYER TRACKER

Days	Prayer Request	Answered prayers
Day 1		
Day 2		
Days 3		

Day 4		
Day 5		
Day 6		

Day 7		
Day 8		

Day 9		